Hudson Taylor

Could somebody pass the salt?

The true story of Hudson Taylor
and a bowl of soup

Catherine Mackenzie
Illustrated by Rita Ammassari

Hudson Taylor lived in a little English village with his father, his mother and his two sisters. They lived in a time when you travelled by coach and horses to get to places and it took you ever so long to get anywhere.

Hudson Taylor lived in a little English village.

One day, something that should have happened quickly took a very long time. Everyone was having their lunch. Hudson was hungry, but he hadn't been given any soup. His mother had forgotten him. Hudson's tummy rumbled, but nobody noticed. He sighed – just a little one – but nobody heard. What would Hudson do?

Hudson was hungry, but he hadn't been given any soup.

He was not allowed to speak at the dinner table. He had to be quiet. He wasn't allowed to raise his hand at the dinner table. Hudson had to sit still. He wasn't allowed to whistle or wriggle or do anything but eat. And Hudson couldn't eat as he hadn't been given any soup!

Hudson was not allowed to speak.

So Hudson just sat and listened. His father was talking about China. In that country there were big rivers, high mountains and wonderful people with long flowing cloaks and jet-black hair. ‘Even the men wear their hair in plaits,’ his father exclaimed ‘and the women have very tiny feet.’

In China there were big rivers and high mountains.

Hudson's father told them about how the Chinese were very clever, and had made wonderful inventions. 'You can see amazing animals there, breathtaking scenery and beautiful plants but they don't have Bibles,' Hudson's father sighed. 'Who is going to tell the Chinese people about God?' he asked.

'Who is going to tell the Chinese people about God?' he asked.

Hudson didn't know the answer to that question and besides he was still waiting for his soup. Just then he had an idea. 'I am allowed to ask for the salt,' Hudson remembered. When he asked for it his mother looked at his empty plate and gasped. Quickly she ran into the kitchen to fetch him some soup.

'I am allowed to ask for the salt,' Hudson remembered.

Just as he finished his soup he remembered something. Hudson remembered that the Chinese people didn't have Bibles. 'How will they find out about God if they don't have Bibles?' Hudson wondered. Someone would have to bring the Bibles to them he decided.

'How will they find out about God if they don't have Bibles?' Hudson wondered.

Many years later, Hudson was walking down a busy Chinese street. His short blonde hair was now long and black. His smart English suit had been replaced by a beautiful Chinese robe. It was market day and the town was very busy. There were lots of people and lots of animals, and Hudson had a job to do.

Hudson was walking down a busy Chinese street.

He bowed politely to an old man on the corner of the street and sat down to speak to him about Jesus. The old man's eyes shone and he smiled when he heard that God loved him. Before he left Hudson handed him some paper with beautiful Chinese writing on it. The old man could now read about Jesus for himself.

The old man could now read about Jesus for himself.

'It is amazing,' thought Hudson. 'When I was little I was worried about not getting my soup. But so many Chinese people have not heard about Jesus. That is something very sad indeed. I hope things will change soon.' Hudson walked back through the market. Other people needed to know about Jesus too.

Hudson walked back through the market. Other people needed to know about Jesus.

Other people did hear about Jesus, lots of them. Hudson Taylor worked hard for many years. Lots of Chinese people know and love Jesus now. But there are still many people who haven't heard about him.

Lots of Chinese people
know and love Jesus now.

For all the boys and girls at Kingsview.
Now that you've heard that Jesus loves you
– it's time to tell the world!

Reprinted 2008, 2012, 2014, 2016, 2017, 2020, 2022 and 2025
ISBN: 978-1-84550-111-2

Published by Christian Focus Publications,
Geanies House, Fearn, Tain, Ross-shire, IV20 1TW,
Scotland, U.K.
www.christianfocus.com

Cover design by Daniel van Straaten
Printed and bound by Imprint, India

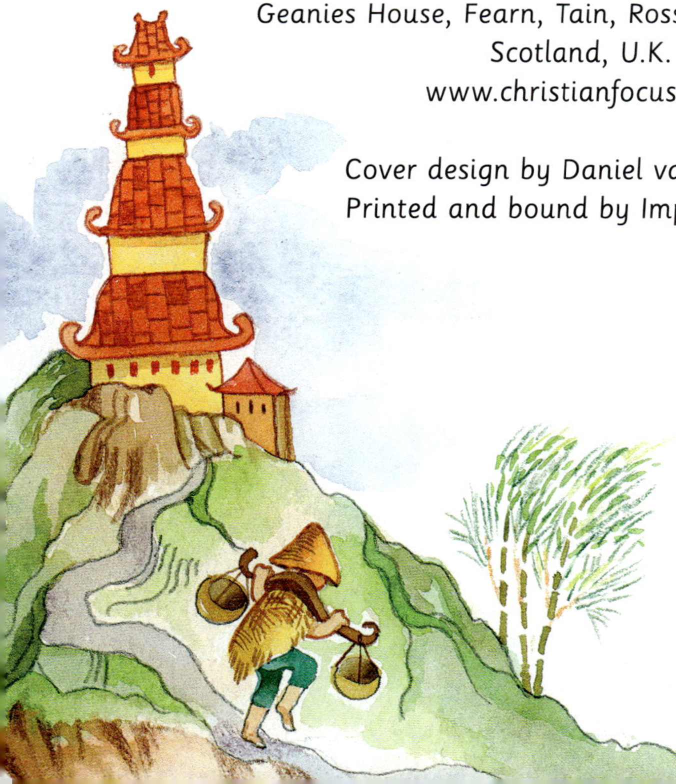